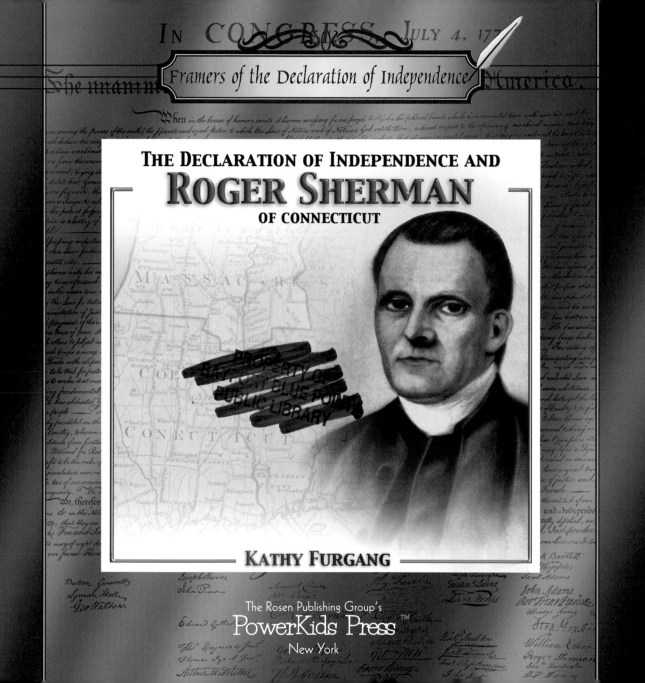

THE DECLARATION OF INDEPENDENCE AND
ROGER SHERMAN
OF CONNECTICUT

KATHY FURGANG

The Rosen Publishing Group's
PowerKids Press™
New York

For Lesley

Published in 2002 by The Rosen Publishing Group, Inc.
29 East 21st Street, New York, NY 10010

First Edition

Book design: Maria E. Melendez
Project Editor: Emily Raabe

Photo credits: Cover and Title page, Map of Connecticut, p. 11 (Map of New England) © CORBIS; Portrait of Roger Sherman and the Declaration of Independence document, p. 4 (Portrait of Roger Sherman), p. 7 (Country-Store Scene), p. 8 (Yale College), p. 12 (Opening prayer of Continental Congress, Philadelphia 1774), p. 15 (All the signers of the Declaration of Independence), p. 16 (Yorktown: Surrender of British commander Cornwallis to Washington), p. 19 (Inauguration of Washington), p. 20 (Village church in autumn, Chester, New Hampshire) © North Wind Pictures.

Furgang, Kathy.
    The Declaration of Independence and Roger Sherman of Connecticut / Kathy Furgang.— 1st ed.
        p. cm. — (Framers of the Declaration of Independence)
Includes index.
    ISBN 0-8239-5593-1 (lib. bdg.)
  1. Sherman, Roger, 1721–1793—Juvenile literature. 2. United States. Declaration of Independence—Signers—Biography—Juvenile literature. 3. Legislators—United States—Biography—Juvenile literature. 4. United States. Congress—Biography—Juvenile literature. 5. Connecticut—Politics and government—1775–1783—Juvenile literature. 6. United States—Politics and government—1783–1809—Juvenile literature. [1. Sherman, Roger, 1721–1793. 2. Legislators. 3. United States. Declaration of Independence—Signers. 4. United States—Politics and government—1783–1809.] I. Title.
    E302.6.S5 F87 2002
    973.3'13'092—dc21   00-011794

Manufactured in the United States of America

CONTENTS

1	Young Roger Sherman	5
2	Roger in Connecticut	6
3	Roger as a Leader	9
4	Fight for Freedom	10
5	Work to be Done	13
6	Declaration of Independence	14
7	Freedom is Coming	17
8	A New Government	18
9	Religious Freedom	21
10	A Good Man	22
	Glossary	23
	Index	24
	Web Sites	24

Roger (shown here as a young man) was very interested in religion, math, law, and politics.

YOUNG ROGER SHERMAN

A great man in American history was born on April 19, 1721, in the **colony** of Massachusetts. His name was Roger Sherman. Roger's father was a farmer. After only a few years in school, Roger had to quit to help his family with the farm. Roger also learned how to be a shoemaker. Even though he had to leave school, Roger never stopped reading and learning on his own. While he worked as a shoemaker, Roger would keep a book open in front of him so that he could study.

ROGER IN CONNECTICUT

Roger's father died in 1741. Roger had to work even harder to earn money for his mother and younger brothers. In 1743, the family moved to New Milford, Connecticut, where Roger's older brother lived. Roger made the journey to Connecticut on foot, with his tools on his back.

Roger became known in New Milford as a smart and honest man. Even though he was only 24 years old, he was **appointed** to posts in the town government. Roger studied on his own and became a lawyer in 1754.

In Connecticut, Roger quit working as a shoemaker. He joined his brother in running a country store, like this one pictured here from the 1700s.

This is Yale College in Connecticut in 1784. Roger gave money to the college to help build a chapel.

ROGER AS A LEADER

Roger's wife, Elizabeth, died in 1760. Roger and his seven children moved to New Haven, Connecticut, where Roger married a woman named Rebecca Prescott. Roger and Rebecca had eight children. In all, Roger had 15 children!

In New Haven, Roger opened another store and worked for Yale College. He became more involved in public service and politics. Roger **represented** New Haven in the government of the Connecticut colony. He was also a judge in Connecticut.

FIGHT FOR FREEDOM

At the time that Roger and his family were living in Connecticut, the king of England ruled all of the colonies. The colonists had to follow his laws. In 1774, leaders from the colonies began to get together to talk about England. Some people were loyal to the king and wanted to work out their problems with him. They were called loyalists. Roger was not a loyalist. He believed that the only way to be free was to make a total break from England. The people who wanted freedom from England were known as patriots.

This is a map of New England in 1755. The colony of Connecticut is outlined in blue.

Although the Second Continental Congress (shown here) was not sure that it wanted a war, the members did agree that the colonies needed an army to defend themselves against the British. George Washington was chosen to lead the troops

WORK TO BE DONE

In 1774, leaders representing all of the colonies gathered in Philadelphia for the First **Continental Congress**. At that meeting, Roger told the other **representatives** that the colonies might have to go to war with England to win independence. He was right. By the time the Second Continental Congress met in 1775, the **American Revolution** had begun. At the Second Continental Congress, the group could not make a decision about whether or not it was a good idea for them to become free from England forever.

13

DECLARATION OF INDEPENDENCE

In June 1776, the members of Congress met again, and a decision was finally made. The American colonies would **declare** themselves free from England's rule. Congress chose Roger to be one of five men who would put together a paper called the Declaration of Independence. The Declaration would explain the colonists' reasons for wanting independence. The other men chosen were Thomas Jefferson, Benjamin Franklin, John Adams, and Robert R. Livingston.

In the center of this drawing are the five men chosen to create the Declaration of Independence. All of the other representatives who signed the document are pictured around the center.

This picture shows the British general Cornwallis (far left) surrendering to American troops at Yorktown.

FREEDOM IS COMING

On July 4, 1776, the Declaration of Independence was approved by the members of Congress. It was a day of celebration. The colonies were going to become a new nation. Congress sent the Declaration to the king of England to show him that the colonies were serious about becoming independent states. Generals read copies of the Declaration aloud to their troops fighting in the Revolution.

The American Revolution would continue until October 19, 1781, when the British **surrendered** after a battle in Yorktown, Virginia.

A NEW GOVERNMENT

The new government in America needed a system. No one wanted the president of the country to have as much power as the king had in England. Roger and other members of Congress decided to split the government into three groups, called **branches**. Each branch could vote and help make decisions for the country. The president would also get a vote, but he or she would never have all the power. Each colony also needed its own **constitution**. Roger helped to write the constitution for Connecticut.

In this picture, George Washington is being sworn in as
the first president of the United States of America.

This is a modern-day village church in Chester, New Hampshire. Even today, many countries do not allow freedom of religion. In the United States, people are free to practice religion as they wish.

RELIGIOUS FREEDOM

Roger was a **religious** man. He studied **theology**, and he often read to his children from the Bible. Roger didn't want to make anyone else practice his religion, though. He believed that the United States should allow everyone to practice whatever religion they choose. One of the most important ideas of the new country of America was the idea of religious freedom. This freedom was not allowed in many countries in the 1700s. In England, people had to follow the religion that the king practiced. In America, people were given their religious freedom.

A GOOD MAN

For the last years of Roger's life, he was the mayor of New Haven, Connecticut. Roger was popular during his lifetime. At one of the meetings of Congress, Thomas Jefferson pointed Roger out to another representative. Jefferson said, "There is Mr. Sherman of Connecticut, a man who never said a foolish thing in his life." Another representative said about Roger, "Roger Sherman had more common sense than any man I ever knew." Roger died in New Haven on July 23, 1793. He was 72 years old.

GLOSSARY

American Revolution (uh-MER-ih-kan reh-vuh-LOO-shun) Battles that soldiers from the American colonies fought against England for freedom.

appointed (uh-POYNT-ed) To be named or chosen for a position.

branches (BRANCH-ez) Sections of the U.S. government.

colony (KAH-luh-nee) An area in a new country where the people are still ruled by the leaders and laws of their old country.

constitution (kahn-stih-TOO-shun) The basic rules by which a state or a country is governed.

Continental Congress (kon-tin-EN-tul KON-gres) Meetings of the colonial representatives held in Philadelphia in 1774, 1775, and 1776.

declare (dee-KLAIR) To make a statement.

religious (ree-LIH-jus) Having to do with God or worshiping God.

represented (reh-prih-ZEN-ted) To have voted or spoken for a group of people.

representatives (reh-prih-ZEN-tuh-tivz) People chosen to vote or speak for others.

surrendered (suh-REN-derd) To have given up.

theology (thee-AH-luh-jee) The study of religion.

INDEX

A
Adams, John, 14

C
Continental
    Congress, 13

F
Franklin, Benjamin,
    14

J
Jefferson, Thomas,
    14, 22

L
Livingston, Robert
    R., 14
loyalists, 10

N
New Haven,
    Connecticut,
    9, 22
New Milford,
    Connecticut, 6

P
patriots, 10
Prescott, Rebecca,
    9

T
theology, 21

Y
Yale College, 9
Yorktown, Virginia,
    17

WEB SITES

To learn more about Roger Sherman and the Declaration of
Independence, check out this Web site:
http://Colonialhall.com/sherman/sherman.asp
http://www.law.emory.edu/FEDERAL/conpict.html#indep